Quickly Grow Your Healthcare Practice

Stop wasting thousands
and start making millions

MICHELE SMITH

Introduction

Many independent healthcare practices will struggle to grow, and many will waste hundreds of thousands of dollars on marketing that does not work. Our team guides healthcare practices across the United States in marketing and growth. Throughout these past 14 years, I have witnessed healthcare practices fail and others have incredible success. I know why some fail and why some thrive. The most exciting discovery and the main reason for writing the book lie in the last step. I hope you find the stamina to read all the way to the end to find out. This book was written to help eliminate some of the mistakes we see on a daily basis. Running a healthcare practice can be extremely difficult, and it can take a heavy toll on your life, your relationships, and even your health. The good news is that it doesn't have to be hard. If you follow each of the steps outlined in this book, you will find rest. You will find peace. But most importantly you will find predictable growth that allows you to build a practice much bigger than yourself. The steps will also help you to avoid wasting hundreds of thousands of dollars on marketing that doesn't work. These are just six of the steps you can do short term to grow your healthcare practice. If you want to engage them all, give us a call (404) 905-1000 and we can get your practice on the path of growth.

— MICHELE SMITH

Don't Spend Another Dollar on Marketing

Before you spend another dollar on marketing your healthcare practice read this entire book. This book will save you hundreds of thousands of dollars in the short term and millions in the long term. The truth is that most healthcare practices will waste at minimum 50% of their entire marketing spend and some attempts will waste 100% of spend without fail. This waste compounded with interest represents millions of dollars for the lifetime of the average healthcare practice. Over the past 15 years we have met hundreds of marketing agencies that churn out creatives, make beautiful websites, and place media ads that cost hundreds of thousands of dollars without even blinking an eye. These creative agencies charge big bucks and sadly most of that money will be wasted. We believe that it is wrong for a marketing company to charge you money and produce no return on investment. We are the firm called in to develop a healthcare practice growth strategy that actually works after the money has been wasted. Your marketing does not have to be complicated. It just has to be executed in a manner that works.

Imagine for a moment that you knew exactly how much money you spent on marketing since you started your practice. Now imagine you knew exactly what percentage of that money was wasted, not providing any momentum at all for your growth or building your brand in anyway. What do you think the truth would be? The truth will scare you and make you furious. It should. Now imagine that you will continue to throw thousands or hundreds of thousands of dollars away every year. Over a lifetime of a traditional healthcare practice the total amount wasted will be millions. How can you prevent this from becoming your future?

This book goes over six steps that you should immediately put into place to start growing your healthcare practice. The book is designed to be a quick read with short chapters that will give you good concrete advice to start growing your practice and stop wasting money. The chapters are:

Step 1 – Know Your Potential Patients – this chapter provides the foundation of everything moving forward. The first step in any marketing program is accurately defining who the potential patient is and what motivates them when it comes to money, emotions and fear.

Step 2 – Fix Your Message – this chapter addresses the fact that most marketing messages are too complicated, too hard to understand and most readers have no idea what you are talking about. Would you send all your marketing out written in Latin? Of course, you wouldn't but healthcare practices do it every day.

Step 3 – Fix Your Practice Perception – this chapter addresses the second step in any marketing program which is ensuring your digital reputation is optimized and managed. Spending money on marketing when your practice has a poor online reputation is just madness.

Step 4 – Fix Your Marketing – Are your goals to grow your patient count or build a healthcare brand? If you focus on the second without focusing on the first, you will quickly run out of money. In today's 24/7 hyper content world, your marketing has to acquire patients.

Step 5 – Treat Your Patients Like Your Mom – Everyone tells you to treat your patients like your mom, but very few people actually understand what that really means. This chapter solves that problem and will even repair your relationship with your mom if you follow these principles.

Step 6 – Stop Listening to the Blind Guide – Did you know you are following the advice of a person who is most likely wrong 50% of the time or more. Worse than that you have been listening to them your whole life. This chapter allows you to stop following the blind guide and get an experienced healthcare practice growth team that can help you reach your goals and not waste all your money.

Conclusion – Wrapping it all up we summarize everything we discuss and urge you to put next steps into place so that you can stop wasting your money, grow your healthcare practice and reach your goals. Simply choosing to use a marketing company that focuses on performance data analytics tracking the correct key performance indicators can not only stop you from wasting millions of dollars, but it can also make you millions of dollars in multiples over a much shorter time frame.

Many people will buy the book, fewer than that will read the book and a small percentage will actually take the steps it outlines and begin growing their healthcare practice. You will be shocked to learn why that is.

Contents

Step 1
Know Your Potential Patients

Before we ever write a letter or begin with the first sentence there are a couple of things we have to know. Who are we writing and why are we writing them? Without those two pieces of information, we would waste countless time writing meaningless letters that were sent to no one and no one would read them. Sounds silly doesn't it. Would it be silly if those letters to no one that said random things were printed on the most beautiful paper you could imagine and held the most beautiful graphics that would make your mouth drop. Sounds like an enormous waste of money for a letter to no one that said nothing in particular. In fact, a large majority of marketing today is thousands of dollars spent on beautiful creatives like graphic design, websites, ads, Facebook and more that are just that. The creatives are sent to everyone which is essentially no one. The creatives actually say nothing as the copy is normally too complicated to understand. And yet we become disappointed after the thousands of dollars spent results in very little effect at growing our healthcare practice. The answer to this dilemma is actually common sense and you will feel a little foolish at your past marketing attempts after you learn the secrets.

When running a healthcare practice, it's natural to focus on our side of the transaction. This means staying focused on the internal aspects of our practice. Items such as scheduling, staffing, product stock or documentation, and more. Many times, we see each patient as the same—just another patient who chose our specific healthcare solutions.

The truth is there is a lot happening on the other side of the transaction. If you are going to grow your practice, every aspect of it has to be patient-focused and not practice-focused. Whether you recognize it or not, your practice naturally attracts a certain patient demographic. This attraction is because of the healthcare you offer or the way you offer it. The attraction is also due to where your practice is located, the population surrounding it and how long it takes to get there. Defining who your organic target demographic is can help you to grow that demographic, take a dominant market share of that demographic and expand into new untapped demographics.

As a general rule, several descriptors are used to define the various aspects of who a patient is. The first is age. As a society, we like to categorize people into groups based on their year of birth, and these groups are known as generations. Knowing which generation uses your healthcare solutions can determine a lot about how you market to them. Here are the generations that occupy the majority of consumers as they are categorized by age:

Baby Boomers I
Born: 1946–1954
Age in 2020: 66–74

Baby Boomers II
Born: 1955–1965
Age in 2020: 55–65

Generation X
Born: 1966–1976
Age in 2020: 44–54

Millennials
Born: 1977–1994
Age in 2020: 26–43

Generation Z
Born: 1995–2012
Age in 2020: 8–25

The first thing you are going to do by default is to think you know how each of these generations engages healthcare solutions. What I can tell you is that you have to look at the research before making a conclusion. Even the Baby Boomer I generation and older demographic are very active adopters of digital technology, cloud-based software, and social media. We have encountered a lot of practice owners who will state, "My patient base is made up of older patients; they don't use the internet." This could not be further from the truth.

If that were true, every practice would still be marketing in the yellow pages. The truth is that the practices that measure results through data analytics have learned that traditional marketing techniques are not working. They have discovered that even their older patients are using the internet to research physicians, locate practices and book appointments.

Social class and income constitute the second important demographic. Higher-income individuals make healthcare decisions differently than lower-income individuals. The factors that affect these decisions are cash-based purchases and healthcare out of pocket limits.

The social classes are generally defined as follows:

Upper Class—makes up about 1% of the US population and is generally considered to comprise those that inherited wealth or "old money."

New Money—makes up about 15% of the population. Includes those whose higher income has only been for a generation or two. Members of this class usually earn their money rather than inheriting it.

Middle Class—makes up about 34% of the population. Includes those who make their money usually working at professional jobs such as engineers, doctors, or lawyers. This group is sometimes also referred to as "white collar" as they generally wear suits or sports coats to work with button-up oxfords or practice casual attire.

Working Class—makes up about 30% of the population. Includes those who make their money usually in a more technical job such as electrician, plumber, carpenter, etc. This group is also known as "blue collar" as they usually wear uniforms to work rather than suits.

Working Poor—It's difficult to determine exactly what percentage of Americans make up the working poor category. It's estimated at approximately 20%. This group often works two or more part-time jobs and receives no health insurance or benefits. This group is most affected by the economy and is generally "last hired, first fired."

Anyone below the working poor is considered to be in "poverty." Estimates state that as much as 13.5% of Americans live in poverty. These individuals usually receive public assistance and do not hold regular employment.

TIP: In order to expand into other demographics, you have to tailor your message to target them by identifying what fears they may have that you need to address and what appeals to them.

Now your first reaction should be, "Wait a minute. If you add those percentages up, it's more than 100%." The truth is that these percentages are constantly in a state of flux depending on the economy and unemployment rates.

Many practice owners will market their health care services without regard to the income levels of potential patients in their geographical market. Lower income individuals who have employee sponsored high-deductible health plans (HDHPs) are more likely than higher income individuals to post pone or forgo healthcare.[1] As a general rule a lower income individual will spend much higher percentages of income toward out-of-pocket medical costs. Your marketing message may have to thoroughly explain how the benefits of the health care outweigh the short-term financial sacrifice. Higher income patients in comparison generally value time over potential costs. Making sure your message communicates how your practice understands how important the time cost is when receiving healthcare could produce a message that resonates with this demographic more than benefits over costs.

The truth is that the best results for marketing a practice are found when you clarify your message to address any potential fears and target your message based on your geographical income demographics.

Performing the data analysis of the demographic make-up of the patient response within a 30-mile radius of your practice can pay dividends in terms of marketing response. Knowing these demographics plays a large part in knowing who your potential patient is and what marketing message is likely to get better results based on addressing potential fears and targeting needs or desires.

Patient Consumer Needs

For the most part, we break down consumer needs into two different categories: desires and needs. Either the patient engages your healthcare service as a need (I have no choice) or a desire (I would like to). While this is an excellent guide in drafting your marketing message and method, the truth is that it's much more complicated than that. As you break down needs and desires, the lines start to blur a little.

For example, the "need" for achievement causes the consumer to strongly value personal accomplishment. This consumer is more likely to choose premium healthcare products or services that they would associate with what a "successful" person would purchase. Seeing these premium brands around them on a daily basis fulfills their personal need for achievement.

This need for achievement can also cross the income class. An example of this would be when a working-class consumer chooses a premium healthcare offering and uses credit cards or financing to make the purchase. A great example would be cosmetic surgery. The need for achievement for this patient is greater than the need to make smart economic decisions.

Another example would be the need for affiliation. The need for affiliation is satisfied by assimilating with groups such as team sports, shopping malls, neighborhoods, networking groups, social media influencers and more.

A larger view of healthcare consumer needs can be explained by looking at Abraham Maslow's Hierarchy of Needs. The hierarchy explains that patients must meet the lower-level needs before they can begin to even contemplate the higher-level needs.

Knowing how patient consumer needs affect consumer behavior can help you to use the right message to attract the right consumer. Knowing that your healthcare product or service mostly appeals to upper-class, Baby Boomer consumers who are seeking self-actualization can be used to create a very effective marketing message.

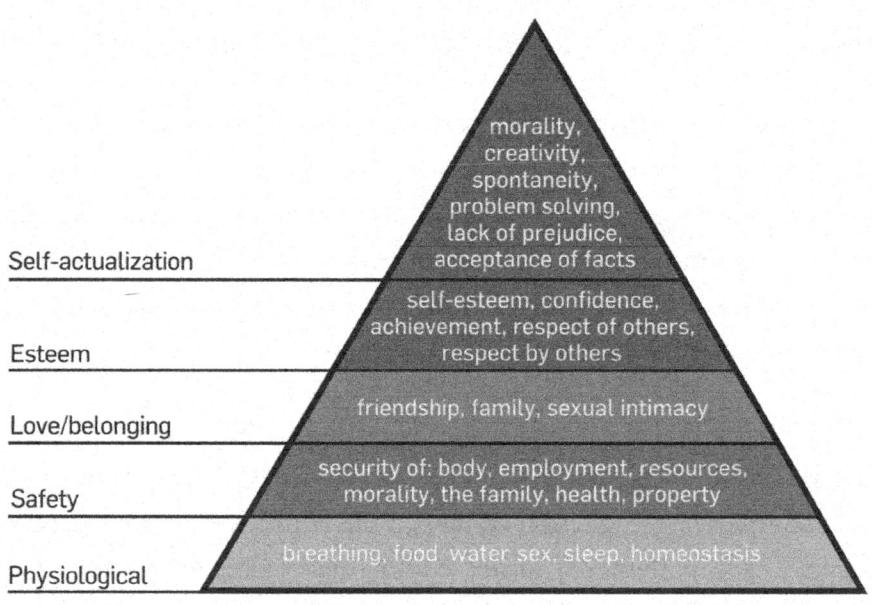

It can also tell you where to advertise that message as you look for marketing channels that appeal to that unique demographic.

TIP: Appealing to the patients' emotions during the patient journey can have an enormous effect during the process.

The Basics of Patient Consumer Behavior

Patient Consumer behavior is the processes or behaviors involved when someone selects, purchases, uses, or disposes of healthcare related products and services to satisfy needs or desires. The most important concepts for healthcare purchases are needs versus desires.

The purchase decision is driven by how the product or service will satisfy a patient's needs or desires.

A healthcare need is something I don't necessarily want to buy but I have to because I need it. An example of this might be physical therapy.

When a patient engages in physical therapy services it is usually to satisfy a health insurance requirement to move to the next level of care or an attempt to try to avoid the next level of care (orthopedic surgery). In this situation the patient will engage in short term care with repeated visits to engage in therapy sessions that patients as a large part do not have time for nor do they particularly enjoy.

A healthcare desire is something I want to buy because I feel some social or emotional transformation or assimilation will occur as a result of the service. An excellent example of this would-be Lasix eye surgery. The patient consumer could easily continue to use eyeglasses, but they are engaging Lasix surgery in order to gain an emotional or social transformation. An example would that they think they would be more attractive without glasses. Or Sarah at the office is so pretty and she does not have glasses. In this situation the most effective marketing message is one that focuses on the emotional or social transformation rather than the details and specs of the surgery itself. When you sell Lasix, surgery based on how it will make someone feel, that becomes highly effective and resonates at a deeper level with the patient consumer. You are not selling laser shaped retina.

You are selling the gift of sight without the trouble of mechanical correction.

Based on defining who the patient is, whether the purchase is a desire or a need and how your product or service fills either of the two should drive your ad message, the design, and the medium through which you choose to send it out to the world.

Think of marketing a need as trying to market an emergency room for a hospital. I can run ads about the soft comfy waiting chairs, the daylight fluorescent lighting, or the nice, sanitized room smell, but none of this is going to connect with the potential patient. When someone needs an emergency room, they are concerned with two things usually: What is the closest hospital? And how long is the wait?

Think of marketing a desire like trying to market the achievement of a higher social class. I can talk about the specifics or the future health improvement benefits all day, but until I paint the picture of how great you will feel after you reach that pinnacle, you are not motivated to engage.

> TIP: Patients buy healthcare according to what they want or what they need; are you selling wants or needs or are you selling anatomical alterations?

The Patient Consumer Decision Process

When making a healthcare purchasing decision, consumers use a very complex process. In a process called constructive processing, they tend to evaluate the effort required to make the choice. They then adjust the cognitive effort required to get the job done based on the size of the decision. When making a very critical or large healthcare decision, they will put in the cognitive effort to get the job done. However, when the decision is considered small or insignificant, they will make decisions using quick, low cognitive processes such as "choose what I always choose" or just make a "gut" choice.

When we break this process down a little further, you can usually divide patient consumer behavior based on three different processes. The first is cognitive. These decisions tend to be deliberate, rational, or sequential in nature. An example of a cognitive-based decision process might be when you are choosing a new neurologist for a chronic disease. Choosing the correct one is very important and would require a large cognitive load when researching the options and making the decision. Offering no obligation initial consultations can help alleviate some of the perceived fears of a potential patient. Letting the patient know that they can come and ask questions and meet the physician before committing as a patient allows a larger group of patients to make the purchase decision since the risk is reduced. This holds true for many patients who are considering any new healthcare providers they have not experienced before. For a lot of patients making the appointment is considered the commitment stage. Many will lack the fortitude to change doctors after the initial appointment unless the patient is extremely unhappy. Due to this hesitation of change, many potential patients could be moved closer to commitment if you provide them permission to make that change without consequence through a no obligation initial consultation.

The second decision process is known as habitual. The patient consumer will make a habitual decision if the cognitive effort is considered low in decision-making. This is where the consumer purchases based on behavioral, unconscious (gut), or automatic decisions. An example of this would be using the same dentist your family has always used. This is a low cognitive decision that is strongly affected by behavioral patterns. A good example of this effect in marketing is when companies offer free samples at the grocery store or at a point of sale. Again, by giving a risk-free option to try a different behavior, the consumer is more likely to break with tradition and at least try a new soft drink.

The last decision process is known as affective. This is an emotional or instantaneous decision process. Emotional decisions are usually wrapped in some past experience or behavior of the consumer or a desire to be affiliated with a different social class or group. For example, choosing to buy a candy bar at the register of a convenience store when you have had a tough day would be an example of an emotionally driven consumer behavior. This is also why you always see options of candy bars or other items at the point-of-sale register. Affiliating your healthcare service with one of these affective decisions can be effective in resonating with the potential patient and the struggles they face.

> TIP: Think of every fear a patient may have about buying your healthcare product or service and then address those fears in your marketing.

Knowing whether purchase decisions for your healthcare related product or service are driven by cognitive, habitual, or affective processes can help you design your marketing message and method to reach your potential healthcare consumers. Define what the cognitive process most likely is for each demographic and then help the patient through the journey by addressing their perceived fears and risk.

Patient Consumer Perceived Risk

When making a healthcare related purchase decision, every patient consumer has one or more perceived risks. This means the patient consumer believes there may be negative consequences if they choose the wrong physician or service. While many of these fears may seem trivial to you they are very real to the potential patient.

Is this practice an honest practice? Are they going to take advantage of my lack of knowledge and rip me off? Who is this physician can I trust him? What about my kids or my daughter? Are they safe with this physician? While this at first seems a little exaggerated, you have to remember that the potential patient has no idea who you are or who your practice is.

There are generally five different areas of perceived risk:

Monetary Risk: This is a general risk with every purchase, but the risk amount increases directly with the cost of the healthcare product or service. Will this practice lie to me and rip me off like that practice I saw on the news? Are they only after my money? Will I be safe? Do they know what they are doing?

Functional Risk: This is a general risk in which the patient consumer is concerned that there may be an easier or better option for the healthcare service. Can I just do this myself? Can I just order reader glasses off the internet?

Physical risk: This is a risk of physical vigor, health, and vitality. Will the physician hurt me or my family? Do they know what they are doing? Will I have a permanent disability?

Social risk: This is a risk of self-esteem or self-confidence. Will using the product or service make me appear poor, hurting for money, or of a lower social class? Will the neighbors see my van in front of the free clinic? Will the neighbors see my car at the men's health clinic?

<u>Psychological Risk</u>: This is a risk of affiliations and status. This risk is similar to social risk, but much more value is involved. For example, this risk includes high-end luxury goods and services. Will the healthcare product or service make me feel special or will I feel horrible from a bad choice?

> TIP: Every one of your potential patients has perceived risks. Addressing these risks lowers your potential patients' purchase barriers. And there can be quite a few.

Some of these risks are exaggerated just to make the point. Every patient does not have this entire list of fears. But surprisingly, wealthier people have more perceived risks than poor people. Addressing perceived fears in your marketing can go a long way to ease a healthcare consumer perceived risk.

Identifying and understanding the various perceived risks that every demographic perceives is critical to crafting your marketing message. If you can identify and address these risks in your marketing message, you can improve your healthcare consumers' purchase frequency, thus making your marketing more effective and more affordable.

First, we define who it is we are talking too. Then we must then define the why. What is the goal? What are we asking them to do? Think about your last marketing campaign and what it said. Would your potential patient instantly know who you are, what you do and what you were asking them to do? If not, then it's time to learn about fixing your message.

Step 2
Fix Your Message

What makes a great marketing message? Its more than just correct spelling, grammar and punctuation. There is one secret about your marketing message that can save you and make you millions. I have a challenge for you that is going to change your life. Starting now I want to look at every marketing message that your encounter. Every billboard, every TV commercial, magazine ad, post card, etc. For every one of these I want you to answer three questions, what does this company do? How does that help me? How do I buy this product or service? After you answer those three questions, I want you to then estimate how much money you think the company wasted on this marketing or if you think it worked. Then imagine the millions of dollars that are wasted every day on ineffective healthcare marketing.

You are going to be shocked at the results. One of the biggest mistakes I see in healthcare related marketing is unclear messaging. Many times, I read healthcare related copy and I have no idea what they do or what they were trying to say. I recognize some industry buzzwords or specialty speak but other than that it just never really says anything. It becomes very apparent that the potential patient was never really considered when architecting or executing the marketing. If you are a physician and you are writing or designing your marketing, stop. The barriers to physician patient communication continue to erode and that communication occurs face to face.[2] Believe it or not writing clear and effective medical marketing copy is quite challenging. The first step is realizing who the reader is.

If you clarify your message your patients will listen. The current problem is that most practices spend a tremendous amount of marketing money that will have very little impact and its due to bad messaging. Most of the marketing has absolutely zero content that actually makes your potential client want to engage your healthcare services. How many times have you launched a new marketing program with anticipation of the results and then nothing happens? A lot of work went into the design. You had multiple meetings with the creative team. You had enormous input into what the campaign would say and how it would execute. You were sure it would be fantastic. And then not much happened. A lot of money transferred from your checking account to the agencies checking account but other than that not much happened. The truth is that most agencies are a team of creatives. They create great websites, they create looking brochures, they have great creative office spaces, everything is just so creative. Creative does not communicate. Creative does not convey. Creative does not convince. Creative does not relate. Creative is not why patients buy health care.

Creative is so important, when paired with the right message. Potential patients buy healthcare when they have heard or read words that persuade them to engage. Patients engage in healthcare when you talk about healthcare in a way that connects with them, emotionally, intellectually, spiritually and fearfully. Patients engage with healthcare options when those options are clearly and effectively communicated in a manner that is important to them. Patients engage the most with healthcare options that are most effectively communicated. Potential patients walk around and move around in a world that is self-centered. Patients only pay attention to things that can help them survive and thrive. Our brains attempt to conserve energy all day long. If your creative does not direct connect with a patient and how it helps them survive and thrive then they very quickly disregard the creative. Most likely before they have even seen 1/3 of the full creative. Our patient's brains have become very effective at weeding out non-important information. The rise in mobile devices and the constant bombardment of information has made the ability of our brains to disregard unimportant information much more powerful. If you do not quickly communicate how your healthcare has benefit to make the patient thrive and survive then your communication is rapidly disregarded in a quick fashion.

As a result, we have to effectively communicate to our patients about how we help them survive and thrive in such a clear way that they do not have to exert any energy in order to recognize and understand this connection. The clearest communication wins, not the best creative. Patients engage in the healthcare they can understand the fastest. When your marketing uses long technical or hard to understand language, your patient is moving on. Quickly disregarding your message and your creative. The more complicated the message is, the less effective it is in engaging a potential patient. If a physician has written or directed the writing of a marketing communication, I can almost guarantee that it is too complicated or holds complex paradigms as it relates to healthcare. Your marketing message must contain simple concepts communicated in a clear manner that quickly relate to the health, happiness and survival of your patients.

> TIP: Having a clear message is 50% of your marketing. Putting that message where your ideal patient can find it is the other 50%. Missing one of them is why most marketing is ineffective. "Half the money I spend on advertising is wasted; the trouble is I don't know which half"
>
> — JOHN WANAMAKER

Presenting Your Message

Your potential patients engage with healthcare related products and services when they quickly tell the patient how they will help them survive and thrive. This means when you are architecting effective marketing communication you must consider how each message is presented. Part of that thriving for your patient is having emotional feelings that relate to happiness such as content, accepted, powerful, peaceful, optimistic, confident, hopeful, valued and more. The non-verbal design of your message is what conveys these emotions. A picture of relatable demographic with a large smile in a beautiful park will convey that emotional response much better than a technical infographic of the digestive system or the anatomy of the eye.

When you present your message with highly technical copy combined with highly technical infographics you are probably engaging the world speed record for potential new patient message disengagement. It is most likely going to be measured in milliseconds. Compare that to a message that is presented with a smiling patient playing frisbee in the park with the copy, "get out and have fun, you deserve it" for patients with irritable bowel syndrome. How much more effective would the simple message that is presented in an emotional evoking wrapper be received than an infographic of the intestines with "suppressing oligosaccharides can help improve your irritable bowel syndrome". In the first message I understand how this healthcare related product can help improve **my** life. In the second I quickly wonder what in the world is an oligosaccharide and quickly move on. The second requires way too much effort for a brain that is trying to conserve energy. The moral to the story is that creatives help convey the emotional response, but they cannot initiate it without a clear and quickly understandable message.

TIP: "If you cannot explain it simply, you do not understand it well enough".

— ALBERT EINSTEIN

Clarifying the message is the most difficult process of the entire marketing effort and the area that most of the effort should be placed. The message has to convey exactly what you do, evoke an emotional response if able and then clearly state how to engage or purchase the product or service. You would be shocked at how many healthcare related websites we evaluate for practices and you cannot find out how to book an appointment, or how to find or buy the product. The websites have a tremendous amount of complex technical communication for the type A personality to get lost in for days on end, but even the best attempts of engaging the service are unrewarded. You have approximately 5 seconds or less to tell the web visitor exactly what you do and how they can engage to receive the product or service. If any part of this takes too long or is too confusing, they will move on very quickly. With the growth of connected mobile devices and the competition for the viewers' attention you can no longer use decades old marketing techniques to convey your message. Your message has to be clear, fast and relatable or else the new human response is to move on at lightening speeds. Anything less is wasted marketing money. There one secret about your marketing message that can save you and make you millions is that every marketing piece has to tell the potential patient what you do, how it helps them survive or thrive, and how they can get it. That simple secret will make your healthcare related marketing incredibly effective.

The marketing is not just about getting the right message out, at least half of the marketing is about how your potential patients perceive your practice. We will find out more about this in the next chapter.

Step 3
Fix Your Practice Perception

How do you find everything patients are saying about you online? There are a number of people that do not like you. They do not like you as a person, they do not like you as a physician, and they do not like your practice. It does not really matter what you do, they are outraged at what happened at them at your clinic. Almost 1 in 5 people suffer from some sort of mental illness.[3] Everyday people leave a fantastically detailed account of a horrible incident that they experienced at a healthcare clinic, that in fact never happened. Have you considered what someone would think about your practice if they thoroughly researched you online? What would they think? What would they tell a friend about your practice? What would they take away from your online reviews? What if the small percentage of your unhappy patients had a brief moment to tell every potential patient what they think about you as a physician or your practice before the potential patient makes the appointment? They are. You are losing hundreds of potential patients just based on your practice perception. Left unchecked it will kill your practice and help waste most of your marketing budget. Does it happen to every practice or just to the bad ones?

Your online reviews are one of the primary ways potential patients lower their perceived risks. Every interaction you have with a patient and their version of how it happened is now being stored across the internet. It has now become so cost-effective to store large amounts of data that it actually costs less to just store everything than to take the time to sort through it to delete what is unnecessary. What this means is that your practice's reputation is being affected by what your patients type all across the internet. And it is everywhere, not just your Google reviews. Think about everywhere your patients might be on the internet on a daily basis.

There are over 60 social media sites that are considered "mainstream" as indicated by daily users. Practice review listing sites such as Yelp easily number over 55. Your practice is getting reviewed multiple times by some of the patients you encounter. It can be a full organized review with a star rating and a brief description of your interaction, or it can be as simple as a reply to a friend on social media who asks if they know someone who knows....

Your online reputation today is important since this is where potential patients are making a large percentage of their purchase decisions. Seeing your practice and physician reviews plays a very large part in whether these potential patients choose to use you.

Now you can see how important your online reputation is. This should change how you interact with patients, going forward. It is very expensive to overcome a poor practice reputation through marketing. In contrast, if you have excellent practice reputation with great employees, you will experience better results at lower marketing budgets. With automated review generation services, you can dramatically increase both the number of reviews your physicians and practice receive as well as the star rating for each review. In general, most of your patients will leave excellent reviews **when asked to do so**. In contrast a small percentage of your patients will leave horrible reviews and some for really minor issues. So, if you do not use a reputation management system you will slowly build a good number of horrible reviews.

Your Brand Perception

You must always remember that your patient knows very little about you or your practice. The truth is they don't really care much about your practice. So patients will sort your practice against others as they search for them on the internet. The sort is a very complex process that is influenced by the consumers' subconscious feelings, perceived fears, potential risks, and how quick they can get an appointment.

The sort generally places all the potential practices into four different categories:

7. **No:** Too risky

8. **Maybe No:** If they are the only one with an appointment by Friday, I might give them a chance, but I still have perceived fears.

9. **Maybe Yes:** Something I saw or heard concerns me but most of my perceived fears were addressed. I will choose this option if a faster appointment is available.

10. **Yes:** Looks like a great practice; all my perceived fears have been addressed. Now if they have an appointment by Friday, we're good.

Now there are two very important things you must remember about the sort. The first one is that the lower the income level of the potential patient, the more likely they are to choose a riskier option. So, you will have lower-income potential patients choose practices from category 1 based off of appointment availability. Higher-income patients are shopping for high quality healthcare and their goal is to remove all perceived risks in the practice sort process.

If you are a great practice but you have lower reviews, then you will fill your schedule with lower-paying patients. Higher-income earners will not want to wait until your schedule opens if you have long wait times. These patients will choose a similar great practice with more availability. This is called lost opportunity cost. If your practice is located in a higher income demographic, then you should carefully consider reserving 1-2 slots each day for new patients. Once you get the high-income patients past the first visit, they are more likely to be flexible in scheduling future visits.

> TIP: If you are setting appointments for new patients further than 1-2 weeks out then you are losing a tremendous amount of the potential patients you are trying to gain and wasting a lot of marketing money.

The other aspects that affect your healthcare brand perception and are very important are:

1. Clean practice walls free from scratches, dents and damage to drywall with fresh paint.

2. Electrical outlets, switches etc, that have broken covers, damaged parts or exposed wires.

3. Dirty or disrepair flooring.

4. Dirty old or disrepair seating, exam tables furniture.

5. Handwritten labels on room equipment, misspellings, tape labels – get a label maker.

6. Outside landscaping – have pine straw beds refreshed twice a year and have landscaping kept and neat.

7. Outside wall siding that is in disrepair or needs fresh paint.

8. Tape adhesive on walls, windows, doors from old handmade signs that were eventually taken down.

9. Fish tanks that were a good idea initially but now look like the swamp thing lives in there.

10. Magazines in the lobby that are 10 years old.

While these things have absolutely no relation to the quality of the healthcare the patient receives at your office, all of these things quickly lower your brand perception. If your patients show up and they see the above, then they are less likely to continue with your practice and will never refer you. When everything is in tip top shape the patient feels like you are more successful, you can be trusted, and they have made a good choice for a healthcare provider. Perception is 100% of your practice brand to your potential patient.

Every practice will suffer some level of impact from poor perception from potential patients. The level of this impact will strongly determine how well you manage this perception. It can either be minute or devastating. Using an active reputation management system can help raise your number of reviews and your average review. But a small percentage of potential patients will only read the bad ones anyway (people love drama). The key to managing poor reviews is to avoid them through the use of the 10 commandments of patient interaction in step 5 and trying to ensure no patient ever leaves a visit or a phone call angry.

How do you find everything patients are saying about you online? The truth is it takes a tremendous amount of time and effort to thoroughly research your practices online perception. The best way to combat this is through reputation management and get the good reviews to way outnumber the bad. Does it happen to every practice or just to the bad ones? It happens to every practice. If you do not have a reputation management plan in place for every physician and your practice you will eventually have a reputation problem that is hard to overcome. The only reviews that happen organically are the bad ones. If you want the good ones you have to ask for them consistently.

Once you have taken steps to manage your practice perception it's time to tell the world about your practice, but first you have to fix your marketing. We will learn about this in the next chapter.

Step 4
Fix Your Marketing

Would you be angry if you learned all of your marketing was showing in a small town in Sicily Greece and your practice is located in Southern California? What if your website would only show to the residents of Sicily? While this sounds unlikely the truth is that a similar issue is occurring with your marketing right now. It is not reaching the right audience. There is one factor that is the most important in your digital marketing than any other by far.

One of the critical factors of growing your practice is getting your clear message in front of your potential patients. Healthcare marketing is changing at a rapid rate. What worked yesterday does not work today. The key to navigating these land mines is to partner with a marketing agency that is data focused and has healthcare related marketing experience. The more experience the better. Healthcare is a very unique industry for marketing. In fact, healthcare can have a high cost of patient acquisition and having ineffective marketing can wipe out even the best budgets. If you hire just any local marketing agency that does not have healthcare marketing experience, you are going to spend about 4 years and hundreds of thousands of dollars training them as they learn from their mistakes. You will know if you hired the wrong marketing practice if you tell them it's not really working and they start quoting web statistics to you such as "unique clicks," "bounce rate," "time on page," and more vanity metrics. If any agency is marketing your practice to maximize traditional web stats, then you are going to waste many thousands of dollars and your patient acquisition rate will be no more than if you had no marketing whatsoever.

Your Marketing Budget

The most effective way to market any healthcare related product or service is to create an effective campaign and then let it run continuously uninterrupted for 5-7 years. That means that you have to be able to afford the marketing. The marekting also has to have enough budget to reach enough people with the right message. Attempts at rapid patient acquisition by setting super high marketing budgets is not sustainable. You have to set a marketing budget that is higher enough to be effective but low enough to be maintainable. If you set a super high budget that you have to cancel in 6 months, then you have wasted six months of marketing. You should budget 4–6% of your gross revenue for marketing. This level should be one that you can maintain, it does not eliminate the profitability of the practice and it enables longevity which greatly improves overall campaign effectiveness. A 5-year campaign will have a much lower cost per patient acquisition based on averages than a 12-month campaign.

Patient Acquisition vs. Branding

When it comes to marketing your practice, it's important to distinguish between patient acquisition and branding. Patient acquisition improves your short-term financials while branding improves your long-term financials. A practice with less than $3.5 million in revenue ($150,000 in marketing spend) should not be utilizing branding. People remembering the name of your practice will not pay the bills. However, if you are spending $150,000+ in patient acquisition marketing, then branding can help make your marketing more effective.

This means your patient acquisition rates will be higher, and this lowers your actual cost per patient acquisition.

The New Patient Funnel

The stages that a patient goes through to engage in healthcare related products and services is different than traditional sales funnels. When a patient is considering new healthcare products or services there is a longer patient education process but a shorter patient commitment process.

Your healthcare marketing strategy should contain both top-of-funnel and bottom-of-funnel tactics. We generate curiosity with new services or techniques that the potential patient may not be aware of. We also generate curiosity with awards, accolades or recognitions that the physicians or the practice receives. We move the potential patient through the funnel to engagement by providing the clear and concise educational material that potential patients recognize how the practice and or the physician and help them thrive and survive.

Keeping your patient demographics in mind, you must utilize different messages for different potential patients by using different channels of communication. To get the process to work at its maximum efficiency and at its highest conversion is very complicated. It takes about 6–8 months for even the most experienced healthcare marketing companies to get the machine running. Every year after that, the process just gets better and better as the machine runs.

Using unexperienced marketing companies can mean little to no results for quite some time before you realize a change needs to occur. Almost 100% of the healthcare marketing programs we take over from other marketing programs are wasting money at a pretty steady clip.

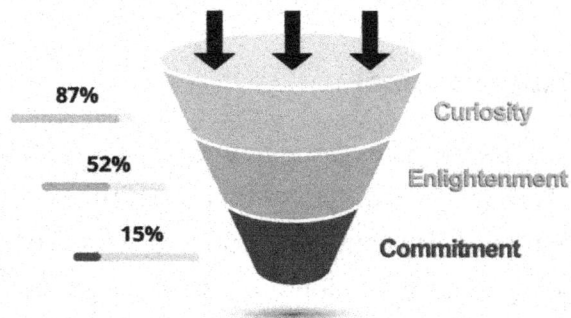

87% Curiosity

52% Enlightenment

15% Commitment

Clarifying Your Funnel Message

It's important that you carefully craft your message with one that is clear and relates to your potential patients' needs at each step of the funnel. Asking a potential patient to choose you as their healthcare provider is asking that patient to enter into a relationship agreement. Just like forming any relationship the process has steps that must be followed. Compare this relationship formation to that of choosing a spouse. It would be awkward to meet someone on the first date and immediately ask them to marry you. There are social rules that outline this process. The potential marriage relationship moves forwards through stages as you get to know one another, what you believe in, what you like, how many kids you want, until you reach the stage that agreeing to marry this person would be a yes. The same relational process occurs when a potential patient is choosing a healthcare provider. The process is much shorter, but the stages are similar. You have to skillfully move the potential through the new patient funnel by being intentional but clear with your marketing messages. An example would be to target potential customers by targeting digital marketing on keywords such as "can't see far way" in the curiosity stage. You then use proven strategy and messaging to move them to the enlightenment phase of keyword targeting of "treatments for nearsightedness". And then gently move the patient to the commitment phase by targeting keywords such as "doctor of ophthalmology near me". By targeting each phase of the potential customer journey with carefully designed marketing you can catch potential patients no matter what stage of the funnel they are on. You can catch them at the curiosity phase and move them gently through the funnel or you can catch them at the commitment phase when they are activity seeking doctors in their area.

> TIP: Your patients have no idea what you do, what ophthalmology means, or what services you offer or why they need them. By focusing on each stage of the patient acquisition funnel you more effectively move potential patients to committed patients.

Many times, potential patients have no idea what you do, what your specialty is about or who to call for what health related problem. If the knowledge you hold about your practice is a level 10 when you attempt to make it simple for them, you bring it down to about a 7 or 8. In reality you need to bring it down to about a 1 or 2. Transforming your message from a 7 or 8 to a 1 or 2 that is clear, concise and relatable and moves the potential patient through the funnel is what an experienced healthcare marketing guide like Oak Healthcare Marketing can help you do.

Picking a Geographic Target

Your geographic marketing area should be comprised of three zones:

+ Your Dominant Area: You will spend the majority of your marketing in an attempt to dominate this area. Usually this is within a 20-mile radius of your practice, depending on demographics.

+ Your Message Area: You will extend your message into this geographic area when the demographic of a marketing channel is larger than my dominant area. For example, if a magazine is delivered to your target demographic but its distribution is larger than your dominant market. Usually this is within a 40-mile radius of your practice, depending on demographics.

+ The No message Area: You will spend money to send a message to this area. This is usually outside 40 miles of your practice and any money spent here would be wasted. Potential patients generally will not travel this distance (there are always exceptions).

When it comes to paid patient acquisition, marketing should target your dominant area, and your dominant area should always include the actual location of your building as the geographical center. We have found that a good radius around your office is 20–30 miles, depending on population and demographics.

Google will prefer your website and online marketing over other practices if you are closer to the potential patient. This will make your marketing more effective and cost less money.

The inverse is also true. If you try to market your practice in places further away from your practice, it will cost you more money and the marketing will be less effective. This is a great strategy to use after you have dominated your dominant area. That is how you grow a practice. But choosing to hopscotch an area to focus your marketing in an area further away from you does not make much sense. The best solution to grow your geographic footprint outside of 30-40 miles is to open a second office in the area that has been identified to most match your demographic target.

Your Website

Hosted websites come is basically two flavors: secure and not secure. You can tell which one it is by the uniform resource locator (URL) in the web address. Basically, if the web address is **http://www.somedomain.com**, then the site is unsecured. If the URL is **https://www.somedomain.com,** then the site uses an SSL certificate and it's designated by the "s" at the end of http in the URL.

So why does this matter? Google set a deadline of July 2018 as the date on which Google Chrome will begin explicitly warning searchers if a website is unsecure. Google is also strongly suggesting that websites be secure when used as landing pages for pay-per-click (PPC) advertising. Both of these strongly hint that SSL certificates are currently playing a role in search engine optimization (SEO) and will most likely play a very large part of SEO in the future.

The SSL certificate also lets the browser know that the website contains verified information and that searchers are actually communicating with your website rather than a pirated copy that was created just to steal user data.

It's highly recommended that if you do not have an SSL certificate installed on your website that you get one. If your current marketing firm has not reached out to you recently to talk to you about getting an SSL certificate, then get another marketing firm.

Either way, the goal is to get the SSL installed and active on your site as soon as possible. It's a big deal.

Are You Mobile-Enabled?

The explosive growth of mobile phones over the last decade has created an issue with website design and development. Even with all the talk on the internet about the importance of mobile-enabled websites, we still talk to potential healthcare clients every day who do not have a website that is mobile-friendly.

So, what does it mean to be mobile-friendly? Your website should be designed in such a way that it detects when someone is accessing it on a mobile phone and then serves that device an altered version of your website. This altered version should be designed in such a manner that the text is easier to read, the menu and links are easier to use, and the images shrink down to the proper size in proportion to the screen-appropriate size.

To determine if your website is mobile-friendly just go take a look at it on your mobile phone. If it's just a shrunken version of your current site that you have to zoom into to read, then your site is not mobile enabled.

So, what's the big deal? Why does it need to be mobile enabled? In 2009, only 7% of all internet traffic was generated through mobile phones.[4] In 2020, that number grew to 50.3%. As the internet speed and technology of mobile phones improves, this number is just going to go up.

Also, page load speed plays a very large role in search engine optimization (SEO) or how well a website ranks on Google. The faster a relevant page loads, the higher it ranks on the search engine results page (SERP). A mobile-enabled website will outperform a non-mobile-enabled site in SEO every day of the week. A mobile-enabled site has a much smaller footprint and size. This means it will load much faster than a non-mobile-enabled site.

Based on our analytics, mobile devices are taking a majority share of PPC advertising. This means that if your website is not mobile-friendly, then Google is choosing not to show your PPC ad to over half of your potential patients.

At the end of the day, it doesn't make any sense to spend any effort in improving the SEO on a website that will lose half its potential audience due to not being mobile enabled. If your site is not mobile-friendly, then it's time to visit an overhaul of your website and discuss how to fix this problem sooner than later.

Local Search Marketing

There are generally two different types of companies. One that sells products that can be shipped to anywhere in the world and one that is bound by geography in some way. In a healthcare practice, we are bound by geography. In pharmaceuticals there is no geographical boundary. This means if you have a local practice, we have to maximize local search marketing.

The competition for local search marketing is getting stronger every year. Practices that have traditionally used local search marketing are increasing budgets and more and more small practices are beginning to participate.

This increasing competition for local search marketing means that marketing companies must use and try new methods in order to produce historical results and similar budgets. As more and more new companies enter the channel, we are also seeing that clients now don't fully understand local search marketing or digital marketing in general. Here are some general facts to help educate you on local search marketing.

Currently, proximity appears to play the most influence on Google local search results. In other words, the closest practice tends to gain the best search engine results page (SERP) spot dependent of the practice's average rating.

As the Google Local Search platform is growing in scale and importance, many internet searchers will call your practice and never actually visit your website. Call-only ads and text ad call extensions mean that Google is functioning more like your practice' homepage. Google is now displaying more and more information about healthcare products and services without actually sending the searcher to the practice website. This means Google is effectively taking your information, re-serving it and potential patients may engage with you without ever leaving the Google SERP.

Websites do still matter but more and more webpages are being designed to improve Google's quality score rating rather than providing information to potential patients. If the high-quality score from your website lets your ad rank higher, then the patient clicks to call you on their cell phone directly from the SERP. While your website played a part in the process, a small number of potential patients will never actually land on the site to read the content or experience the usability.

Another very important aspect of your SERP ranking is your Google practice reviews. There appears to be a very strong correlation with the number of reviews and the average review rating as it relates to SERP placement.

Local search plays a very strong role in healthcare. Understanding and maximizing that your local search profile can significantly increase your leads while providing a generally lower cost per lead.

Keywords

Keywords are what Google and the other search engines use to connect internet searchers who are looking for healthcare services with your website. These keywords are very important and are the separator between an experienced healthcare marketing practice and a local marketing firm that markets many different types of companies.

Let me give you an example. If I were hired by a bakery today to market their practice, I would do some keyword research, build the website, and start the PPC marketing. I know nothing about running a bakery. But I would assume the keywords would be "cakes," "wedding cakes," "birthday cakes," etc. I would then do some keyword research online and gather a large set of bakery-related keywords and put my marketing plan into action.

Let's reverse that example and let me demonstrate what happens when a local marketing practice starts to market your healthcare service. They take keywords such as "ophthalmology," "ophthalmologist," "optometrist," etc. They do some keyword research online and gather a large set of healthcare related keywords and put the marketing plan into action. What sort of SEO traffic do you think they will attract? If you said, other ophthalmologist looking for health care marketing you would be correct. You would be shocked at the amount of junk traffic you get from high level keywords like "ophthalmologist." An experienced healthcare marketing firm would know that in order to attract potential new patients you have to use longer tail keywords such as "ophthalmologist near me" The differences between marketing healthcare and every other industry are vast. Even if they are a top-notch marketing practice that pays very close attention to data analytics, it will take them 16–24 months to "learn" how to market your practice while they are steadily spending your budget.

Another way to stop junk traffic from eating up most of your PPC budget is through the use of negative keywords. Negative keywords tell Google what keywords we are not interested in showing up for. Keywords like "ophthalmologist marketing," Negative keywords are so important that running a profitable PPC campaign is absolutely dependent on an exhaustive negative keyword list. From time to time, I hear other marketing companies make the comment that PPC marketing does not work for some companies or that it's too expensive. When I hear that, I know that they are not utilizing an exhaustive list of negative keywords. The negative keyword list is so important that we utilize a global negative keyword list that we share across hundreds of accounts. Each time a search term is executed on the internet we analyze the search term the patient used and what keywords triggered the click. When we discover a new needed negative keyword, it gets shared across all accounts. This happens on every search for every account every second of the day.

Another consideration that must be taken into account for health-care related marketing is Bot clicks on your PPC campaign. Bots and fraudulent clicks from competing physicians can eat up your pay-per-click budget pretty quickly. In response we utilize a proprietary software that registers the IP address of fraudulent bots and physician clicks and prevents those clicks from occurring the in future. If you are utilizing any type of pay per click marketing you should utilizing fraud click blocking software.

SEO Timeframes

Search engine optimization (SEO) is using programming, content and meta data to improve a website search engine results ranking for a given keyword. When thinking about SEO it is best to evaluate the results in years rather than months. Search engine experts mostly say that it will take anywhere between 6 and 8 months just to get a new site indexed on the search engine. Gaining true SEO traction also takes a significant amount of time.

When performed correctly, SEO will help boost your website traffic, user engagement, patient acquisition, and your overall internet presence. The absolute best SEO programs will age like fine wine over years rather than months.

The true return of good organic traffic will outperform all other marketing channels in cost per lead after the SEO has reached its full potential.

This is why it is so important to select the right SEO provider from the start. Once you have done your homework and selected a good reputable SEO practice with a proven track record, then dig in. The absolute minimum commitment to a proven SEO practice should be at least 5 years. We are not advocating a 5-year contract but rather a 5-year relationship in which you give the process time to mature.

Some companies jump around from SEO provider to SEO provider after they did not reach number one on Google after 3 months. This is a terrible mistake. If you have chosen a good SEO provider based on strong recommendations, then commit to a long-term relationship. Give the practice at least 5 years and see what great true SEO results are like.

Think of a long-term SEO strategy like the magic of compounding interest in a retirement account. If you moved your retirement account every 3–6 months, you would lose a large sum of money to fees. The same holds true for SEO. Find a great practice. Let them craft a great SEO strategy and then let the practice do its work. Hold on and give the efforts time to mature. An SEO program that uses White Hat SEO techniques with legitimate backlinking takes multiple years. But this type of SEO will slowly mature your site to one of authority and strong organic performance, i.e., clicks that you didn't have to pay for. Why does it take so long? Consider that Google has indexed over 130 trillion websites across the web. Each of those websites have to be "re-indexed" on a regular basis in order to evaluate SEO changes and place the website higher or lower in the search engine results page. That's 356 billion websites Google has to index a day. That's 14.8 billion websites Google has to index an hour. That's 247 million websites Google has to index in a minute. That's 4 million websites a second. Needless to say, it takes a significant amount of computer hardware, computer software, internet bandwidth and server space just for Google to keep up. In light of all those stats, waiting 6-8 months for SEO changes to affect a search results page result does not seem that long. Keep in mind that while they are doing that, they are also collecting and storing a horrifying amount of personal data on each of us. So, in short, it just takes time.

Reading the Analytics

Once you get your website's SEO up and running, it's time to turn to the analytics. The analytics give us the data that tells us how our patients are interacting with the website and we know way more than you can even imagine. Are they staying a while, visiting multiple pages and performing research? At first thought, this may seem like a great thing. But if the goal of the marketing was to generate patients for your practice and your do not get new patients, then the marketing missed its objective.

If you are measuring time on page, click though rate and bounce rate, then the marketing might be successful. It's important to determine exactly what you will consider successful and what your marketing company will consider successful. What do we want the patient to do? This is known as a key performance indicator or KPI.

If you have correctly defined your KPIs, then you can read the analytics and determine if you are meeting the goal.

One of the biggest mistakes I see from other marketing firms is that they get caught up in reading website that measures standard website performance like bounce rate, page sessions, click-through, etc., without any regard for a useful KPI. Just having a website that performs well based on vanity metrics will not pay the bills. The bank will not accept your Google Analytics (GA) monthly summary for deposit.

Here is an example to demonstrate what I'm talking about. Your goal should be to book new patients online through a web form or by the patients calling your practice.

If phone calls are the goal, then a patient that lands on your site, immediately dials the number to book the service, and then clicks off the site, this would be a score for your practice. But traditional web analytics data would show that this session was not effective. Your on-page time would be very small, maybe even counted as a bounce. Your click-through would also be null. But this patient called and booked an appointment. If your marketing company measures this as "bad" and shifts tactics to eliminate the "bad" then your new patient acquisition is going down. This is why defining your KPIs are so important.

> TIP: Paying more for an experienced healthcare marketing firm will pay for itself in higher patient conversion rates (more phone calls) and lower costs per new patient for marketing.

Analytics provide an exceptional amount of data that you can spend hours each week analyzing. You can even get so caught up in the analytics that you lose sight of the forest for all the trees you're looking at. Just because it can be measured does not mean it should be a KPI. Your practice goals are to help your patients and make money, and this determines your KPIs. Just using analytics for analytics' sake can waste a tremendous amount of time and lead you to chase insignificant goals. If a marketing practice keeps quoting website analytics such as bounce rate and page sessions, when you keep telling them it's not working, then you need to pick a different marketing firm.

Previous Patients

There are some things that you have to realize if you are going to be successful in marketing your healthcare practice.

There are really only two patient designations: a previous patient and a potential patient. When your marketing is effective your current patients are going to utilize the marketing channels to book appointments. People in general are lazy. They are going to perform a Google search for your practice, click on one of your pay-per-click ads and then book the appointment. At first glance the normal visceral response would be this is not working, and my current patients are costing me a lot of marketing money. The truth is that this cannot be stopped, the more effective the marketing becomes, the more your current customers are going to use it. If you are going to be successful in long term practice growth strategies, you are going to have to focus on new customer acquisition numbers and disregard previous patients that use your marketing. If you attempt to stop this, you will gut your marketing program and you would be better off just stopping the marketing all together. Previous patients are going to use the marketing.

Returns on Digital Marketing Spend

In the early days of digital marketing, it was easy like shooting fish in a barrel. There were more and more patients looking for healthcare companies on the internet every day and there were very few healthcare providers using the internet to market. The PPC was literally 25 cents per click.

That 25 cent click in 1997 now can cost as much as $147 per click in 2020 if you don't know what you are doing. This means that the cost is going up even for those of us that do know what we are doing.

The most common error that occurs with digital marketing is matching your expectations to your marketing spend. Based on all our data over the last 14 years with hundreds of companies, you should see about a 4-10 times multiplier per spend. So if you spent $40,000 on marketing, you should see $160,000–$400,00 in gross new patient revenue growth. For a small practice, you will see that increase. For a moderately sized ($1–4 million dollars) practice, you might not even notice that an increase occurred.

To determine how much you should be spending on digital marketing, take your gross sales and multiply it by 0.04 (4%).

Why is the return different for each practice? The results are based on a very complicated accumulation of factors and here are just a few:

1. Your competition: How many practices there are there to serve the geographic population.

2. Your population density.

3. Your population-average household income.

4. Your local competition that is utilizing digital marketing. It's not like traditional advertising; the cost of digital marketing is real-time supply and demand. The more the demand, the higher the cost.

5. Your practice's brand perception in the community. If you are a so-so practice with poor ratings and reviews across the internet, the marketing is not going to be as effective for you.

6. The clarity of your message and how well you enabled the buyer's journey. The easier it is to become your patient; the more people will become your patient.

Marketing on Sale

The one thing you must always remember is that if any marketing is on sale it's because it does not work. A billboard, magazine ad, web directory, shopping cart ad, magnet on the front of the yellow pages, or any other marketing method you can possibly think of that actually provides leads and a positive ROI would not be on sale or "special discount" just for today to close the month out. Every marketing program that works is never on sale. It doesn't have to be. There is also never a deadline with the special offer expiring and it requires your purchase decision immediately. If it works, there are enough people in line to use it, and you can decide to use it at your leisure.

For the past 14 years, we continually hear from potential healthcare clients that signed up for this great deal that all the big healthcare companies around them were supposedly using that was half off if they signed up that day.

If the marketing works, it's not on sale. If the marketing firm does what they say they will do, they have a line of people signing up. They don't have to call you over and over or send you expensive gifts.

There are some things in life you just don't buy on sale:

+ Fish

+ A lawyer (never hire a lawyer you can afford)

+ Marketing

"Hello, This Is Google Calling"

Never, never, never sign up for any marketing program, special offer, domain-renewal hosting program, or anything digital-related that is pitched to you over a cold-call phone pitch. Google is not going to call you with an "urgent message regarding your Google Maps listing." Google has literally billions of Google Maps listings with millions configured correctly, millions configured incorrectly, and millions unclaimed. They are not going to take the time to call you about yours.

Telemarketers call thousands of healthcare practices a day and tell them:

+ Your SEO is not performing correctly.

+ Your ads are showing in some other state.

+ Your website has serious configuration issues.

+ Etc. Etc. Etc.

The people calling you on the telephone about anything related to your Google account or your website are just trying separate you from your money. These telemarketers call us on a daily basis as well. We just hang up. We advise you to just hang up as well.

The one factor that is the most important in your digital marketing than any other by far is your website. The website is the absolute foundation for every marketing you attempt. It has to have an SSL certificate, it has to load super-fast, it has to be free of malware and it has to be designed around the right keywords and navigation. Without the right website your marketing will never reach its full potential.

After your marketing is fixed you then have to fix the culture in your practice. There is no amount of marketing budget that can overcome a bad culture or the lack of culture. But a great culture will grow the practice with a minimum marketing budget and will explode a practice with a 4% of gross marketing budget. In order to change the culture, you have to treat your patients like you would treat your mom. We examine this in the next chapter

Step 5
Treat Your Patients Like Your Mom

If you asked me to choose just one of these steps that would have the most impact on your healthcare practice it would be this one. Treat your patients like your mom. This one step will grow your new patient referrals faster than anything else you can do. It will fill social media with post and comments about your great practice. It will fill discussion boards with posts and comments about your great practice. It will unlock a tremendous number of patient referrals. But most importantly it will unlock the most coveted goal of every marketing company and every fortune 500 company. This is the big kahuna and it's what everyone is after.

But what does "treat your patients like your mom" really mean? We hear it a lot. We read it a lot. And after 15 years we have learned that it does not mean the same thing to everyone. Some people treat their mom horribly. Just FYI if your relationship with your mom is trained, use these 10 Commandments and you will have her eating out of your hand in no time.

You have to create a culture in your practice where every person knows how they are to treat every patient at every encounter. This means answering the same question over and over for every patient with care, patience and understanding. It means always having the patient's perspective in everything you do. Go the extra step to help them make new appointments, get appointments at other offices as needed, navigating their healthcare, basically anything and everything you can do to help. Your patients are putting an enormous amount of trust in you and your staff. They have chosen to use your practice for whatever reason, but at the foundation of each of those reasons is that they trust you with their healthcare. Respond to that trust with genuine care. But it's not enough just to say it. You have to build a culture in your practice that believes it. A culture that makes everyone feel it deep to the core in everything they do. A culture that drives them to always do the right thing, even when they are tired, or even when no one is looking. You can't just assume it will happen because they are great healthcare workers. If you are not actively building the culture of your practice, then your staff is. And I can promise their idea of the ideal workplace is not your idea of an ideal healthcare practice. But if the culture is implemented correctly, they will come aboard pretty quick and feel good about what they do every day for work.

In our experience we have found that two items must be defined in order to convey what it means to treat every patient like they were your mother and how exactly to build that culture.

What exactly does it mean to treat every patient like they are your mother? First you have to define how your mother would want to be treated. **The following are the 10 commandments of patient interaction:**

1. Don't criticize, condemn or complain.

2. Give honest, sincere appreciation for the patient.

3. The patient does care how much you know until they know how much you care.

4. Become genuinely interested in your patients' lives and who they are.

5. Smile – everyone longs for happiness, give it freely.

6. Remember to each patient their own name is the sweetest and most important sound in any language. Use it often

7. Be a good listener – encourage your patient to talk about themselves. Talk less, listen more.

8. Always talk in terms of the patients interests.

9. Make the patient feel important and do it sincerely.

10. The only way to win an argument is to avoid one. You may win the argument, but you will never change the mind.

How to build this culture in your practice

Telling everyone in your practice to read the list of 10 Commandments is one thing, actually developing this culture is a whole different ball of wax. The good news is that healthcare workers as a whole will strongly buy in to a patient centric culture. Once you take steps to initiate the new culture you will most likely be surprised at how easy it is accepted and how quickly it will intertwine with the core beliefs of your staff. Your team genuinely wants to come together on a common vision of purpose, patient centric care and success. Today's healthcare workers have high expectations of their employers and are looking for purpose far greater than pay. A 2018 LinkedIn survey concluded that culture is the most important value to today's work force.[5] The survey found that 70% of responders would not work in a company if it meant they had to tolerate bad workplace culture. This was so important that 65% of them would tolerate lower pay and 26% would forego a fancy title if they could have a great work culture.

The great news is that your healthcare team is hungry for a patient centric care defined culture. Building a practice culture really comes down to answering these three questions:

1. Why does your practice do what it does (i.e. why do we exist)?

2. What do we believe (i.e. what are our values)?

3. Where do we want to go with the practice (i.e. what is our vision for the practice)?

All you have to do is take the following steps to integrate the new culture.

Step 1 – define your core values. Using the 10 commandments of patient interaction choose 4-6 core values that will be foundational for your practice. Three are not enough and seven is too many. Five is ideal. The goal of the core values is to guide your team in every decision they make. In order to do this, they must be easy to memorize. These core values will eventually become an intrinsic part of the everyday fabric of your employee and patient experience. After you have defined your patient centric core values then you move on to the next step.

Step 2 – evaluate where your culture is now and if you need to make changes. The most difficult part of step 2 is that you cannot really do the measuring. As you will learn in the next chapter, your bias is going to skew your measurement. If you do the evaluation you will discover that your culture looks more like what you hoped it would be rather than what it truly is. My recommendation is that you get a non-partner staff member or outside third party to perform a culture measurement survey to get an accurate measurement of where you are in regard to your new core values.

Step 3 – define what steps are necessary to move the culture from your current state to one that reflects your new core values. These steps generally include the following:

1. Educate your current employees on what the core values are and give examples of how these values guide behavior and decision making.

2. Educate your current employees on the 10 commandments of patient interaction. Give examples of how each one should be followed.

3. Monitor employee behavior moving forward and give positive feedback every time you see an example of an employee demonstrating the new culture. (avoid negative feedback in front of others, praise in public, criticize in private).

4. Print the core values, 10 commandments of patient interaction and any other supporting statements and post those around the practice.

5. Every time you hold a meeting, discuss a topic, hold an employee performance evaluation, or use a teaching moment, bring it back to the core values. Always mention how every possible item relates to the core values.

6. Incorporate your core values and 10 commandments of patient interaction into your new employee onboarding

process. Make sure potential new employees appreciate and can buy in to your culture and core values.

7. Give yearly awards at your practice annual parties, meetings, etc. that reinforce your core values. Some examples are the founders award – given to the employee that best demonstrates all your core values. The award for each core value – given to the employee that most demonstrates that particular value. Patient Interaction Award – given to the employee that most demonstrates great patient interaction using the 10 commandments of patient interaction.

8. Employee measurement – make sure adherence to core values is a part of your employee review process. In progress discussions and yearly evaluations give each employee honest feedback about their alignment with each core value and how they can improve if needed.

9. Live the core values – You must make your core values central to every ting your practice does, talks about and measures. I cannot emphasize enough how ineffective it will be if you simply print a poster of your core values and hang it on the wall with absolutely no mention of it again. When you bring out your new values, your employees are going to wait and see if this is real or just talk. If you hold firm and totally embrace it, they will get on board. If it's just a poster on the wall, then they will continue with culture as usual.

If you embrace the 10 commandments of patient interaction and you successfully implement and maintain this culture in your practice it will have an incredible impact on your patient acquisition. But most importantly it will unlock the most coveted goal of every marketing company and every fortune 500 company. This is the big kahuna and it's what everyone is after. It is the evangelist referrer. When you get this part right you begin to create evangelist for your practice. With absolutely no pay or compensation they will take it upon themselves to tell everyone they know about your physicians and about your practice. You notice them referring you on social media to people they do not even know. You cannot buy this type of marketing when you get 15-20 evangelist referrers working for you. Imagine having 20 hype men working around the clock to tell everyone they know about you. They also begin affecting other people. Other patients will begin to chime in and sing the praises of your practice and pretty soon recommending your healthcare practice becomes in vogue. It's the style. All the cool people recommend your practice. This is known as the tipping point as it is the most coveted point for any business or healthcare practice. Once you achieve the tipping point, the prophecy of your practice becomes self-fulfilling. This is when you find yourself on the cover of magazines talking about how to grow a great practice and how to deliver great healthcare. It is really not that hard, just takes a consistent earnest attempt at implementing a patient centric healthcare practice culture. If you have dreams of this kind of grandeur the first thing you have to do is eliminate the advice of the person who is leading you astray. This person is known as the blind guide and they are incredibly effective at leading you down the wrong path. You will learn more about them in the next chapter.

Step 6
Stop Listening to the Blind Guide

This is by far the second most important step in growing your practice. This one is so important that you should stop at nothing in recognizing who the blind guide is and stopping their attempt to sabotage your practice. You will never believe who it is and how effective they are at convincing you to do exactly the wrong thing.

Recently, I was at the Story Brand certified guide training in Nashville, Tennessee. During this program, you develop your Story Brand by learning how to clarify your messages. This exercise includes filling out what is known as the Story Brand 7-step framework. In the workshop we pair up as partners with either the person on your left or right. Each participant then works to clarify their own message and then we review the message of our partner and give helpful hints or help. One thing to consider is that the entire group is made up of marketing professionals. Almost everyone at this workshop is in marketing or copywriting. Also keep in mind that I have been writing marketing copy for other companies for over 20 years. I was well versed in the process, and I understood exactly what they wanted me to do. But each time I went to write the copy for my own marketing company, I got too bogged down. The message would get too complicated and my neighbor would always have an enlightening insight that would instantly help me clarify my message. I then noticed that my partner also struggled when writing about his own marketing company. I would have to help him clarify his message and strip out all the complicated unnecessary verbiage. I then got curious and started listening to all the people around me, and I noticed everyone was suffering from the same problem. We could write outstanding copy for our neighbor's message, but we all struggled to write a copy about our own message. Curious about this, when I got home, I began to do some research. What I found was enlightening. It is actually the exact problem that almost every small business or practice is struggling with. It's actually the one deciding factor that made me write the book.

The thing I learned is that we are all listening to a blind guide. When we see others that are following the blind guide, we instantly recognize it. When a healthcare practice similar to yours is following the blind guide, you see it clearly. You recognize how they are getting off course and what they should do to get back on track.

We all follow the blind guide. It's so bad that we are following the blind guide in almost every aspect of our lives! Looking back on every healthcare practice we have consulted with a pattern emerged. In every healthy, successful and growing practice, the owners have reached out and recruited, hired or obtained a cabinet of external experts that guided them in growing the practice. The practices that are struggling are all following the blind guide. When you do not recognize that you are following the blind guide your life becomes frustrating. You get stuck in ruts, your efforts seem to be wasted, and you seem to waste a tremendous amount of time and money learning hard lessons.

The blind guide was discovered by us after we were exposed to a theory of two psychologist. The theory was presented first observed by two psychologist named Joseph Luft (1916-2014) and Harrington Ingham (1916-1995) in 1955. The pair named the theory the Johari's window using a combination of their first names.

	Known to Self	Not Known to Self
Known to Others		
	Arena	Blind Spot
Not Known to Others		
	Facade	Unkown

The window is represented by four panes of glass. Arena or Open refers to the things that others know about you and you know about you as well. The blind spot is things others know about you, but you do not recognize about yourself. Façade refers to the things you know about yourself, but others do not know about you. Unknown are things you do not know about yourself and others also do not know about you.

While the study was conducted using a pre-determined list of descriptive adjectives it also is a great metaphor in describing how the principles of Johari's window can be used to expose the principles of the practice owner making decisions. Leaning heavily on Luft and Ingham's science we now propose the Oak Health Practice Growth Window.

In this window the four panes of glass are almost exact. Arena or open refers to practice growth experience that is held by you and outside experts. The blind spot is practice growth experience that is held by outside experts but not by you. The façade is practice growth experience that is unique to your practice and unknown by the outside experts. The unknown pane is practice growth experience that is neither known by you or the outside experts based on the unique properties of your practice.

When you further examine the Oak Health Windowpanes, half of your practice growth decisions are being made by a blind guide! That blind guide is you! You do not see or recognize what steps need to be put into place for a successful outcome. Half of your decisions will result in wasting money, effort and learning a lesson rather than implementing growth. You're blinded by the trees and can't see the forest. Your emotions sway your logic. You justify decisions in order to justify an end. Why would you take the long hard route of wasting the money and learning the lessons of failure? The only sure route is to recognize your limitations and engage the experts.

After I learned this, the practice growth struggle became clearer. All of my frustrations and questions about how a healthcare practice owner would almost deliberately sabotage his practice growth and waste thousands of dollars of his/her money became crystal clear. The practice is too close to self. The blindness cannot be overcome without the lesson of failure or the use of a guide. Why not choose a guide rather than a hard lesson?

The only way for the healthcare practice owner to succeed is to find great outside guides who have great advice. You must choose outside guides that have a proven track record of growing a healthcare practice. You must then trust and follow the advice of the outside experts.

I see it crystal clear now. All the most successful healthcare practice owners hire outside experts and get out of the way. They don't micromanage them. They know a great guide will see the path of success clearer than the owner ever will. All the most successful healthcare owners' partner with great experts who guide them in growth. The exact same principles apply to climbing Everest. Would you rather risk death and try to figure it out or hire a guide who has successfully climbed the mountain before.

The experience at the Story Brand guide certification training and discovering Johari's window changed my paradigm. I now can usually tell within about 15–30 minutes of talking with a healthcare owner if the blind guide is making all the decisions or if they have engaged outside expert help. Its mostly the first.

It has also changed how I operate, market, and grow my business as well. I now understand I am too close to the trees, and I need a guide. We use great partner guides to help us navigate the rapidly growing aspect of artificial intelligence marketing and programmatic marketing. We use guides to help us scale a rapidly growing healthcare consulting company. We use guides to help our executive leadership learn the behaviors to motivate and lead our team. We have a full cabinet of guides, and the results have been invaluable.

Were you shocked to learn who the blind guide was? Now you realize how effective the blind guide can be in leading you astray. Now that you have the power of this knowledge, the future is really up to you. Will you continue to let the blind guide make the decisions? Or will you engage great guides who will help you grow your practice and change your life?

Conclusion

This book covered six steps that you should immediately put into place to start growing your healthcare practice. The book is designed to be a quick read with short chapters that will give you good concrete advice to start growing your practice and stop wasting money. The take always from each chapter are:

Step 1 – Know Your Potential Patients – Knowing who your dominant target demographic is critical in crafting clear messages that resonate with them. Know who they are, and you know how to push their buttons.

Step 2 – Fix Your Message – After we know who we are talking to, we make that message as clear as possible and we take the comprehension level way down to meet the potential patient and tell them what we do, how it helps them survive or thrive, and how to get it.

Step 3 – Fix Your Practice Perception – You must have a reputation management system in place. Without it you die a slow death.

Step 4 – Fix Your Marketing – Engage smart proven marketing techniques that have proven to be successful for hundreds of healthcare practices.

Step 5 – Treat Your Patients Like Your Mom – Create a patient centric culture and implement that culture. This will pay huge dividends going forward and make your marketing super effective.

Step 6 – Stop Listening to the Blind Guide – Surprise, you are the blind guide. If have not successfully grown other healthcare practices why would you think you are qualified to grow yours? Find outside experts and engage them. You practice healthcare and leave everything to the experts in each field.

Now it's time to put next steps into place so that you can stop wasting your money, grow your healthcare practice and reach your goals. Call us, we can help (404) 905-1000.

Many people will buy the book. Hundreds of copies of this book will be purchased by healthcare practice owners. Hundreds of copies of this book will be given away at our speaking engagements, trade shows, by salespersons, etc.

Fewer than that will read the book. Of those people who either purchase or are given the book only 60% of them will open the book to read it. Less than 40% will read the book all the way to the end.

Less than 20% will actually take the steps this book outlines. So, if you actually read the book, and implement the steps it outlines (or call us) you have a very good chance of implementing real growth at your healthcare practice. When you do this your competition will have no idea what you did or how you suddenly became so successful. Some of them will even have the book on a bookshelf or in their office and still have no idea what you did. When they ask you how you did it, just tell them it's highly complicated.

We have provided you a small glass of milk. We know that you will not buy the cow as long as we provide the milk for free. If you want to stop wasting marketing money and start growing your healthcare practice, give us call (404) 905-1000 and we will guide you on that path.

Endnotes

1   https://www.ncbi.nlm.nih.gov/pmc/articles/PMC4004054/

2   https://jaoa.org/article.aspx?articleid=2093086#:~:text=For%20 example%2C%20the%20Accreditation%20Council,skills%3B%20 (4)%20counseling%20and

3   https://www.nimh.nih.gov/health/statistics/mental-illness.shtml

4   https://www.smartinsights.com/search-engine-marketing/ search-engine-statistics/

5   https://blog.linkedin.com/2018/june/26/workplace-culture- trends-the-key-to-hiring-and-keeping-top-talent